Standin' Tall®
with FORGIVENESS

by
Janeen Brady

Series Includes

1. Obedience
2. Honesty
★ 3. Forgiveness
4. Work
5. Courage
6. Happiness
7. Gratitude
8. Love
9. Service
10. Cleanliness
11. Self-Esteem
12. Dependability

Brite®
Success. It Just Follows.

Hi kids, I have a question for you. Now think really hard and tell me something new you've learned this week.

★ **I learned to spell two new words**

SECOND CHILD: I learned to tie my shoes.

I'm proud of you. Have you ever wondered just how many new things there are to learn?

★ **Hundreds and hundreds.**

SECOND CHILD: Thousands!

 So many things to learn,
So many things to know,
So many things to learn,
So many ways to grow.

I'll bet you've learned many things already. Would you like to show me what you can do. OK.

 Learn to bounce a ball, learn to jump a rope.
Learn to climb a tree, learn to swim a stroke.
Learn to ride a bike, learn to read a book
Learn to pump a swing, even learn to cook.

You know there are different ways to learn things. You can use your mind or your body, and sometimes you learn new things with the feelings deep within you.

★ **With our feelings?**

Oh yes. It's with our feelings we learn to love and to be happy. And it's with our feelings we learn to forgive.

★ **I've heard that word, but I'm not sure I know exactly what it means.**

It's quite simple, really. It means letting go of angry feelings and putting good ones in their place,

 When somebody makes you sad, when somebody makes you sad,
Do you still feel love inside or does love just seem to hide?
When somebody makes you sad, when somebody makes you sad,
Can you treat them kindly? Can you truly forgive?

SECOND CHILD: But it's hard to be nice to somebody who's been mean to you.

I didn't say it was easy. Sometimes it's very hard. But when you forgive somebody, the unhappy feelings go and the good ones come in. It's great!

SECOND CHILD: I'm still not sure I understand.

How can I explain it? I know, we'll make a movie. Would you like to be the star?

SECOND CHILD: Yes.

Okay, listen to the director and do what he tells you. You will play the part of Max.

DIRECTOR: Places everybody! Quiet on the set! Lights, camera, action! This is take one.

All right Max, you're walking to school. There are several boys playing ball and you stop to watch. You'd love to play, so you ask if you can join them.

SECOND CHILD: Can I play too?

DIRECTOR: Good! Now the boys answer.

BOY ONE: Are you kidding? You're too clumsy Max.

BOY TWO: Yeah, you can't hang on to the ball.

DIRECTOR: This makes you very angry Max. Let's see some anger. Grit your teeth. Good! Now clench your fists and make a mad face. Bring in the angry music! Excellent! Show us how terrible you feel Max. Your stomach hurts, your heart pounds and you feel like a big knot has been tied inside you.

Now, one of the boys hits a high, arching ball that sails over the fence and down a steep hill covered with bushes. Okay, read your line Max.

SECOND CHILD: Serves you guys right. Now you've lost your old ball.

DIRECTOR: Try it again. This time get really mad.

SECOND CHILD: Serves you guys right! Now you've lost your old ball!!!

DIRECTOR: Perfect, print it! Thanks everybody, take a break.

★ **Is that how it ends?**

DIRECTOR: Yes, that's the ending.

★ But that's terrible. The movie shouldn't end with Max having all those awful feelings.

 When somebody makes you cry, when somebody makes you cry,
Can you look the other way, can you wear a smile that day?
When somebody makes you cry, when somebody makes you cry,
Can you treat them kindly? Can you truly forgive?

DIRECTOR: Do you have a better idea of how the movie should end?

★ Well, maybe Max can forgive the boys.

DIRECTOR: That's a great idea! Let's go back and change the ending. Places everybody. Quiet on the set! Lights, camera, action. This is take two.

SECOND CHILD: Can I play too?

BOY ONE: Are you kidding? You're too clumsy Max.

BOY TWO: Yeah, you can't hang on to the ball.

DIRECTOR: Max, you feel very sad. You watch the guys having fun and your lip quivers. That's it. Now wipe a tear from your eye. Good! Now the ball goes up over the fence and down the hill.

This is a close-up of Max. Max, you're thinking, "It serves those guys right," but you decide to get rid of your bad feelings and forgive them. Okay, bring in the nice music. Ah, yes.

Now change your expression, Max, from anger to forgiveness. Get rid of that knot inside and replace it with a warm, happy feeling, as if your heart were smiling. Now you smile, Max. Let your face tell the story.

Great ending! Print it!

SECOND CHILD: Wait! There's still something else I could do. I could jump up, climb the fence, slide down the hill and find the ball, then toss it back to the other guys.

BOY ONE: Hey thanks.

BOY TWO: You're okay Max.

BOY ONE: Sorry I called you clumsy.

SECOND CHILD: That's okay.

DIRECTOR: Tremendous! I love it! What a fantastic ending, why didn't I think of that.

You were just great. I'm so proud of you.

SECOND CHILD: I bet those guys feel better too, because they said they were sorry.

You know you're right.

There are two sides to forgiveness, it's important that you know.
Two sides to forgiveness and it always has been so.
One side says I'm sorry for hurting you my friend.
The other 'I forgive you' then hurts begin to mend.

There are two sides to forgiveness and we need to practice both.
Two sides to forgiveness each essential to our growth.
If you should upset somebody, learn to kindly say 'I'm sorry.'
And if someone injures you the kindly thing for you to do is say
  'I forgive, I forgive, I forgive you.'

✱ I think I'm learning about forgiveness. But it's not going to be easy. Oh well, I guess I can forgive a lot of people who make me feel bad.

If you want to be happy you will try to forgive everyone.

✱ But what if they're really mean to me?

When you keep bad feelings inside it doesn't hurt them, it only hurts you. Here's a little story that will help you understand.

One day JoAnn was on her way home from school.

JOANN: Mr. Snyder is cutting down his tree. I've never seen anyone cut down a tree before.

MR. SNYDER: That about does it. She's going...timber.

JOANN: It's a huge tree.

MR. SNYDER: Little girl, what are you doing there, run, run, the tree will hit you, RUN!

JOANN: Oh my leg, my leg hurts.

Luckily only a small branch hit JoAnn, but it hit her so hard it went into her leg. Mr. Snyder carried her home. Her parents carefully pulled out the slivers and cleaned her wound. Each day her leg looked better and it soon healed completely.

★ **How is that like forgiveness?**

You'll see, the story's not over yet. Many days later JoAnn's leg started to swell up and itch as if it were infected. Then one day, when it was hurting especially badly the wound opened and a great big sliver came out. You see, the sliver had been there all the time and it caused the sore.

That's exactly what happens to people who don't forgive.

★ **You mean their bad feelings stay inside of them like the sliver?**

Yes, those feelings grow and fester like a big sore until the person can hardly stand it. And the only way to feel better...

★ **Is to get the bad feelings out — to forgive.**

Exactly.

✸ Now I understand, but what about . . .

Yes.

✸ What about . . . Well, sometimes I get angry at myself.

You get angry at yourself?

✸ Yes, like when I took my brother's bike without asking. I knew better, but I
did it anyway. He was mad at me and so was I. It made me feel awful.

I get angry at myself, I get mad, mad, mad,
When I know what I am doing is bad, bad, bad.
Do you get angry too?
At myself, oh yes I do.

I get angry at myself, I feel blue, blue, blue,
When I'm doing things that I shouldn't do, do, do.
Do you get angry too?
When I'm bad, oh yes I do.

I don't like to think of the times I have failed.
Then I'm afraid to try.
I don't like to think of mistakes I have made.
That only makes me cry.

I get angry at myself, I get cross, cross, cross,
And I feel alone, afraid all is lost, lost, lost.
Do you get angry too?
Oh yes, oh yes I do.

Did you ask your brother to forgive you?

★Yes, and he did too, but I still feel bad.

When you've done something you're sorry for and you ask to be forgiven and you promise never to do it again, there's still one more thing to do.

★What's that?

Forgive yourself.

★Forgive yourself. I've never heard of that. Isn't it hard to do?

Yes it is. In fact it's probably the hardest kind of forgiveness. Many people have a difficult time forgetting their mistakes and forgiving themselves. But it needs to be done if you want to have good feelings.

★How can I forgive myself for taking my brother's bike? He was so disappointed in me. I let him down.

Is there anything you could do to make it up to him?

★Well yes, I could help him with his chores.

That's a splendid idea!

★Hey, I feel better already. I'm not such a bad person.

I still like you.

★Well then, I guess I should too.

 I like me, I'm okay, I'm all right, I feel good about myself.
I like me, I can live with myself and be happy.
I like me, I'm on top, I'm out front, I'm not wasting on a shelf.
I can see I am someone and I like me.

I know I'm not perfect, I've never said I was;
And though I've got a ways to go,
As long as I'm trying, who cares about my flaws?
I'm learning to see the bright side.
It's only smart to see the light side.

I like me. I'm my friend, I'm my pal, and the three of us agree
That we like me.
I am someone worth knowing, I'm growing and
I like me!

The full program on each CD or cassette is followed (side B of the cassette) with the same program but leaves out the lines of the main child in the story, giving the listener the chance to read along, saying aloud the missing lines and actually becoming a member of the cast. This fascinating activity helps older children with their reading and provides an excellent opportunity for development in dramatics.

Children can sing along with the songs, color the pictures and participate in still other activities as the story progresses.

A Product of BRITE MUSIC ENTERPRISES, INC.

Music and Dramatics recorded, engineered and mixed at Bonneville Media Communications.
Illustrations by Grant Wilson and Neil Galloway / Graphic production by Whipple & Associates.
Music arranged and conducted by Merrill Jenson.